# Stegosaurus

BY BARBARA ALPERT

amicus
high interest

Amicus High Interest is published by Amicus
P.O. Box 1329, Mankato, MN 56002
www.amicuspublishing.us

Library of Congress Cataloging-in-Publication Data
Alpert, Barbara.
 Stegosaurus / by Barbara Alpert.
     pages cm — (Digging for dinosaurs)
 Audience: Grades K to grade 3.
 Includes bibliographical references and index.
 Summary: "Describes how the Stegosaurus was discovered,
how paleontologists study its bones, and what the fossil
evidence tells us about this plant-eating dinosaur with plates"—
Provided by publisher.
 ISBN 978-1-60753-367-2 (library binding) —
 ISBN 978-1-60753-415-0 (Ebook)
 1. Stegosaurus—Juvenile literature. I. Title.
 QE862.O65A385 2014
 567.915'3–dc23
                        2012045078

Editor: Rebecca Glaser
Designer: Kathleen Petelinsek

Photo Credits: Corbis, 6–7, 9, 13, 22, 26, 28–29; Getty, cover,
5, 10, 14, 17, 21, 25; Shutterstock, 18-19

Printed in the United States of America at Corporate Graphics
in North Mankato, Minnesota.
5-2013 / 1145
10 9 8 7 6 5 4 3 2 1

# Table of Contents

# A Dinosaur with Plates

The tall grass moved. A big animal, almost as big as a school bus, looked for food. On its back were plates shaped like triangles. A tiny head rose up. Its **snout** was full of leaves. The Stegosaurus looked around. It was safe to eat more.

Stegosaurus ate only plants. It tore off leaves with its sharp beak. Its dull teeth were good for chewing.

Not many dinosaurs tried to attack Stegosaurus. It was too big. It could hit them back with its spiky tail. So most dinosaurs stayed away. But not Allosaurus. He was huge. And he could sneak up and attack at any time!

**Two Allosaurus sneak up on a Stegosaurus.**

7

# The Discovery of Stegosaurus

In 1877, **fossils** were dug up in Colorado. The diggers found bones and flat plates. They sent them to O.C. Marsh. He was a **paleontologist** at Yale. Marsh had not seen fossil plates before. He said they looked like roof tiles. It was a new dinosaur! He named it Stegosaurus, or "roof lizard."

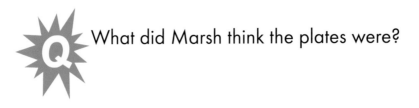 What did Marsh think the plates were?

Marsh's field crew looked for dinosaur bones in the 1870s.

 **Armor.** He thought the plates lay flat on the animal's back.

Some people thought Stegosaurus had only one row of plates.

 Were all the plates the same size?

As more Stegosaurus fossils were found, Marsh studied them. The plates were too small to be armor. It was more likely they stood up. In 1891, Marsh wrote that the dinosaur had one row of plates. But later, others said it had two. No one knew. In 1992, a nearly whole Stegosaurus **skeleton** was found. It proved the plates were in two rows.

 No. The biggest plates were on its back. The ones near its head and tail were smaller.

Marsh was shocked at the size of a Stegosaurus skull. It was tiny. This big dinosaur's brain was only as big as a golf ball! But there was a space at the end of its spine. Did Stegosaurus have another brain to control its tail? Maybe. But later studies showed that it had only one brain.

A Stegosaurus skull was small compared to skulls of other dinosaurs.

The four spikes on the tail of
Stegosaurus are called a thagomizer.

Stegosaurus

Q How do scientists feel when they find
a new fossil?

Scientists looked at the tail **spikes** too. The first ones found had four sharp spikes. They stuck out. They made a good **weapon**. More bones were found. Were they the same? No. Some spikes were much longer than others. Some had spikes in other places. Scientists decided there were other kinds of Stegosaurus.

 Most scientists are excited but not Earl Douglass. In the early 1900s, he was digging for Apatosaurus bones. But he found lots of Stegosaurus bones instead!

# Fossil Clues to Study

Stegosaurus plates are still a mystery. They were not as strong as people once thought. They were not armor. So what did they do? Maybe they helped the Stegosaurus cool off or warm up. The plates had tunnels to hold **blood vessels**. That means they could get colder or hotter.

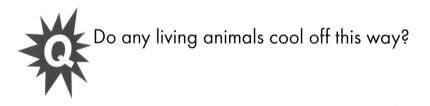

Do any living animals cool off this way?

 Yes, an elephant does. Hot blood goes up to its big ears. The blood runs through blood vessels in its ears and cools. A Stegosaurus's plates may have worked this way.

What else could plates do? Some scientists think the plates were colorful. Bright colors could help a Stegosaurus find a mate. Or maybe they helped the dinosaurs spot each other. There are many fossils to study. But it is hard to prove that any idea is right.

The plates may have helped Stegosaurus cool off in the hot sun.

Stegosaurus's front legs were much shorter than its back legs. Why? Short front legs would keep its head low. Then it could eat plants on the ground. But some scientists think the Stegosaurus stood up on its back legs. Its tail would help it balance. Then it could have eaten tall plants.

Some people think Stegosaurus could stand on two legs.

Before 2007, Stegosaurus fossils had only been found in North America.

# Recent Finds

In 2007, bones were dug up in Portugal. It was the first Stegosaurus found in Europe! This one was shorter than others. But it could have been a young one. Scientists think that long ago North America and Europe were one **continent**. These bones added support to that idea.

Another exciting find occurred in Wyoming. In 2007, an almost whole Allosaurus was dug up. A Stegosaurus was under it. A Stegosaurus leg bone was right next to the Allosaurus's mouth! Scientists think this dinosaur was the main enemy of Stegosaurus. These fossils show they may be right.

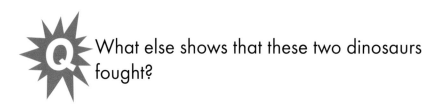

**Q** What else shows that these two dinosaurs fought?

**Allosaurus was an enemy
of Stegosaurus.**

 An Allosaurus backbone was found with a hole
in it. The hole matches a Stegosaurus tail spike.
A neck bone with a bite in it was found. The
bite matches the teeth of an Allosaurus.

# Stegosaurus Today

You can see dinosaurs at the Dinosaur National Monument. This park is in Colorado and Utah. Many Stegosaurus bones have been found there. Some are still in the ground. Many years ago, Earl Douglass thought people would want to see them that way. Every year, many people do.

People work to dig up huge fossils.

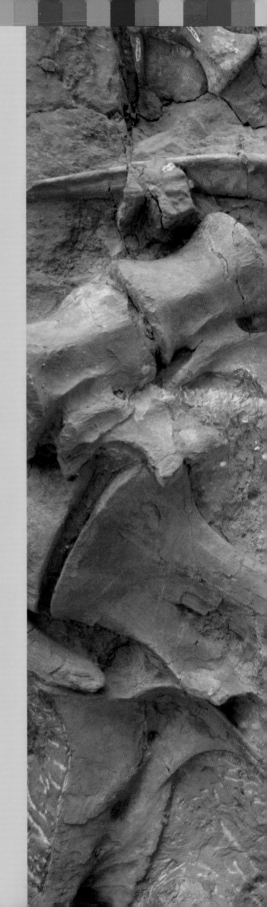

Scientists are still digging. The ground is full of dinosaur bones! At a **quarry**, visitors can watch paleontologists at work. What new fossils they will find?

**Each new find gives clues to the past.**

# Glossary

**armor** A stiff covering that protects something.

**blood vessel** Tube that carries blood throughout the body.

**continent** One of the large land masses on Earth.

**fossil** The remains of a plant or animal of a past age preserved in earth or rock.

**paleontologist** A scientist who studies fossils.

**quarry** A place where rocks and fossils are dug up.

**skeleton** The frame of bones supporting a body.

**snout** A long, narrow nose.

**spike** A long, pointed object; Stegosaurus had bony spikes on its tail.

**weapon** An object used to fight or defend.

# Read More

**Harrison, Paul**. *Armored Dinosaurs, and Their Scary Spikes, Spines, and Horns!* Prehistoric World. London: Arcturus, 2012.

**Mara, Wil**. *Stegosaurus*. Rookie Read-about Dinosaurs. New York: Children's Press, 2012.

**Riggs, Kate**. *Stegosaurus*. When Dinosaurs Lived. Mankato: Creative Education, 2012.

# Websites

**Dinosaur Facts**
*http://www.kidsdigdinos.com/dinosaurfacts.htm*

**KidsDinos.com—Dinosaurs for Kids**
*http://www.kidsdinos.com/*

**Stegosaurus—The Dinosaurs.org**
*http://www.thedinosaurs.org/dinosaurs/stegosaurus.aspx*

**Stegosaurus—Enchanted Learning**
*http://www.enchantedlearning.com/subjects/dinosaurs/dinos/Stegosaurus.shtml*

# Index

# About the Author

Barbara Alpert has written more than 20 children's books and many books for adults. She lives in New York City, where she works as an editor. She loves to travel and has collected fossils in New York, New Jersey, Montana, and Pennsylvania.